GRANDMA WAS HERE!

Bil Keane

FAWCETT GOLD MEDAL • NEW YORK

"It isn't Grandma."

"All right, what's all this quiet about?"

"When little girls get bigger they all seem to grow out of shape like that."

"It's for the bake sale at school, but I can buy
it back if you want me to."

"I got a 98 today!   Miss Johnson took my temperature."

"How can they pack such big flowers into such tiny seeds?"

"Dinner in the yard is just eating outside. For a
REAL PICNIC you hafta get in the car
and go someplace."

"They're homemade flowers from our garden."

"Dear Easter Bunny: Please bring me a large chocolate egg filled with coconut cream, some jelly beans, heavy on black . . ."

"Look, Mommy! An Easter bonnet."

"Mommy, why does your eggnog taste different than mine?"

"Don't worry about it. Ours won't be the only chocolate-covered tax return they'll get."

"Which do you wanna see first, Daddy? My report card, the test paper or the note from Mrs. Gallagher?"

" . . . then we went on the roller coaster . . .
then we ate lunch . . . then we went on the
merry-go-round . . . then Dolly threw up
. . . then we came home."

"When will the flowers start climbin' up their ladder?"

"I got a gold star for attendance, Mommy, and guess where she put it!"

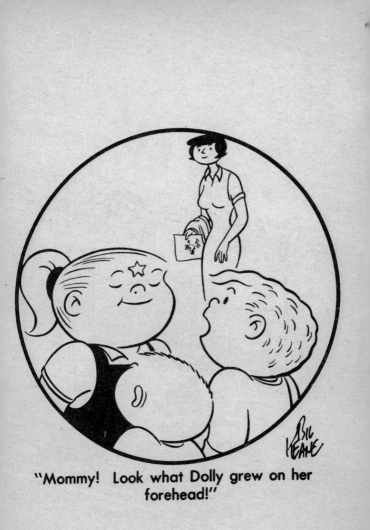

"Mommy! Look what Dolly grew on her forehead!"

"Of COURSE I notice something new, Love.
It's your . . . face . . . your forehead . . .
a STAR on your forehead!"

"You might wash off the star!"

"Couldn't I stay home from school today to go
show Grandma my prize for
perfect attendance?"

". . . and here's a star for you, Jeffy, for picking up your toys, and another one for eating your lunch, and . . ."

"Well! How were things down in the mine today?"

"But, Mommy! I don't know how to work it."

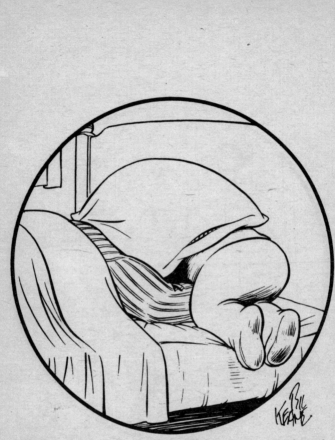

"Why do you have this pillow over your head,
Daddy?"

"My toes love sandals because they can see out."

"Oh, no! You golfed your tee."

"Daddy, why did you tell Mommy you think
they ought to do away with tipping?"

"If I pull this string will it fall apart?"

"Would you like me to show you around
our tent?"

"Look what's in our driveway! A real
live truck!"

"Is that flotsam or jetsam?"

"The morning glories are open for business."

"We've gotta do our spilling outside."

"You can answer that kind of a door without
your pants."

"'Stead of 'love' let's just say 'zero'."

"I win, Daddy! I had 142, and you only had 78."

"That's a good thing about dresses. You can
make a table with them."

"I wish I could fly on a trapeze so I could wear
one of those little shiny silver bathing suits."

"If this one's a fork, is this one a 'THREEK'?"

"Hi, Daddy! Want some mud pizza?"

" . . . and when the flowers are born you'll be their father."

"If you find a golf ball, it's mine."

"One peanut butter and jelly on white, and he'll have a jumbo cheeseburger, french fries and a chocolate shake."

"Are you very busy right now, Mommy?"

"I pushed most of mine downstairs."

"Let's let the rain run awhile till it warms up."

"See? It turns itself into a sliding board!"

"After this one, Daddy . . . No, wait! After
this next one . . . Hold it . . . Now!
. . . No, after the blue one . . .
OK . . . No, wait . . ."

"Will you get in bed with me, Mommy? I don't
like to sleep alone."

"Daddy gets put to bed the same time as us tonight 'cause he's going fishin' tomorrow."

"Arizona got the highest mark."

"Could you use a good hole for anything, Daddy?"

"Billy isn't going into the Army! He's going to a summer camp for a couple weeks."

" . . . and, Dolly, you can play with my robot
and I'll let Jeffy use my skateboard,
and, PJ, you can . . ."

"I was homesick for a while, but I got over it
when the bus pulled out and I couldn't
see my mom waving."

"Why do they call the teachers ` counselors'?"

"Ya mean it's not heated?"

"Even if they ARE all reruns, we're sure missin'
a lot of television."

"Wish my mom was here to make me eat this."

"If we sink, which one of us has to go down with the ship?"

"Mommy! It's a letter from Billy, but it has 15
cents postage due. Do we want to pay it?"

"Dear Mommy and Daddy: Today we have to
write home. Love, Billy.   PS. Don't touch
this letter or you might catch my
ivy poison."

"Do I hafta know any words besides 'giddyap' and 'whoa'?"

"I just remembered — my father already HAS a wallet."

"I shoulda brought my mom's microwave oven
— it's faster!"

"Maybe our folks don't have to pay for
rainy days."

"I'm only allowed to use arrows with rubber
suction tips."

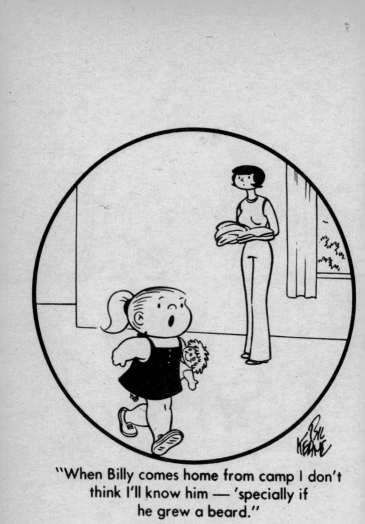

"When Billy comes home from camp I don't
think I'll know him — 'specially if
he grew a beard."

"Please, Lord, just ONE fish? One bite?
A nibble?"

"Please, Mommy? Couldn't I stay
another week?"

"Well, well, little people, been good children
while I was away? By golly, PJ, I believe
you've put on a little height. And, you,
Jeffy my boy . . ."

"Daddy, will you fatten up my horse?"

"I'll show you some of the fish I caught at camp when we unpack my suitcase."

"That noise means it's empty, Jeffy . . .
I said, when it makes that noise it's . . .
Jeffy! . . . Jeffy? . . ."

"Jeffy's gettin' real good. His pitches only bounce once before they reach the plate."

"Wow! This world goes down a long way!"

"Why are all these black specs in my milk?"

"Why can't watermelons have one big seed like peaches?"

"We need them for bases."

"Know what? If you draw a very small
tic-tac-toe thing, it means
'number'."

"My mom's next door and she asked me to bring over her umbrella."

"One of the things Daddy likes 'bout tennis is
the little dress Mrs. Lincicome made for
herself. I heard him tell her."

"Hurry, Mommy! Daddy's racing his engine at us!"

"Is Billy, Jeffy, PJ, Dolly or your father here?"

"We better give Daddy more to eat. I just
beat him arm-wrestling."

"I'm makin' her food and her dress the same color so if she spills any it won't show."

"PJ will be right out of the bathroom. I just
heard Mommy say 'good boy!'"

"I wish you'd mow this rug, Daddy."

"Put some lather on mine, too, please."

"I'm givin' Mommy a spiritual bouquet and
usin' my money to get a catcher's mitt."

"I think you'd do better if you tried NOT
singing to him."

"You'd like this story, Mommy. It has a mother in it."

"I want a lot of outside."

"Mrs. McCall is comin' to sit with us. She's the
one who always bursts into tears."

"Is that new one gonna be his real tooth?"

"It won't fly. All it does is taxi."

"I hurt my elbone!"

"On second thought, let's take a booth."

"Billy! You better hold Daddy's hand so that if
an animal escapes it won't eat you!"

"I wouldn't wanna sit behind him at
the movies."

"If the chimp is the smartest of all the animals
do they pay him the most money?"

"They remember even longer than mommies."

"I bet he'd be easy to ride. Look at the handlebars."

"That's a boa constrictor. He can hug you
to death."

"The sign says 'Dromedaries' but they sure
look just like camels."

"Billy's saving some of his lunch to feed the
animals and that's not allowed!"

"He'd have an awful time gettin' a
sweater on."

"Come back, Dolly. He's not through
looking at you."

"If he's so sly how did he get caught?"

"Jeffy went back to say goodbye to the gorilla."

"How long till dinner, Mommy?"
"One more inning."

"I think maybe Daddy doesn't like it around here. He's always runnin' away."

"Ever since the day you broke your arm fallin'
off your skateboard, I haven't been
able to find mine."

"You'll have to go someplace else to blow
bubbles."

"Daddy's gonna be real surprised when he comes back from downtown. We're washing his license plates for him."

"Babies grow up to be kids after a couple of whiles."

"I think this scale is slow."

"Mommy said rain makes things grow, so I put
PJ out there."

"Where's Mommy?"
"In the house getting control of herself."

". . . a bottle cap, half a scissors, a golf ball, a
doll's arm, a battery, a piece of a yo-yo . . .
this stuff all belongs in Mommy's
junk drawer!"

"Starting now all the months end with 'brr'
because it's getting colder."

"How many 'Back to School' days till Christmas?"

"Can I skip my homework, Mommy? The
teachers went on strike."

"Could you come back later? Mommy's tryin'
to give me a bath."